Dear Parent:

Remember the first time you read a book by yourself? I do.
I still remember the thrill of reading the words Little Bear said
to Mother Bear: "I have a new space helmet. I am going to
the moon."

Later when my daughter was
learning to read, her favorite I
Can Read books were the funny
ones—Danny playing with the
dinosaur he met at the museum
and Amelia Bedelia dressing
the chicken. And now as a new
teacher, she has joined the
thousands of teachers who use
I Can Read books in the classroom.

I'm delighted to share this commemorative edition with you.
This special volume includes the origin stories and early sketches
of many beloved I Can Read characters.

Here's to the next sixty years—and to all those beginning
readers who are about to embark on a lifetime of discovery that
starts with the magical words **"I can read!"**

Kate M. Jackson
Senior VP, Associate Publisher, Editor-in-Chief

EMMETT'S PIG

Pictures by Garth Williams

An I CAN READ Book

EMMETT'S PIG

PIG

by MARY STOLZ

HARPER

An Imprint of HarperCollins*Publishers*

I Can Read Book® is a trademark of HarperCollins Publishers.

Emmett's Pig
Text copyright © 1959, renewed 1987 by the Estate of Mary Stolz.
Illustrations copyright © 1959, renewed 1987 by the Estate of Garth Williams.

Illustration on page 1 copyright © 1963 by Fritz Siebel; renewed 1992 by the Estate of Fritz Siebel. Additional illustrations on pages 68–71: Amelia Bedelia sketch copyright © 2013 by the Estate of Fritz Siebel from *Amelia Bedelia: Fiftieth Anniversary Edition*. Berenstain Bears sketch copyright © 2017 by Berenstain Bears, Inc. Biscuit sketch copyright © 2017 by Pat Schories. Danny and the Dinosaur sketch copyright © 2017 by Anti-Defamation League Foundation, Inc., The Author's Guild Foundation, Inc., ORT America, Inc., United Negro College Fund, Inc. Fancy Nancy sketch copyright © 2017 by Robin Preiss Glasser. Frog and Toad sketch copyright © 2017 by the Estate of Arnold Lobel. Little Critter sketch copyright © 2017 by Mercer Mayer. Pete the Cat sketch copyright © 2017 by James Dean. Pinkalicious sketch copyright © 2017 by Victoria Kann. All rights reserved. Manufactured in China. No part of this book may be used or reproduced in any manner whatsoever without written permission except in the case of brief quotations embodied in critical articles and reviews. For information address HarperCollins Children's Books, a division of HarperCollins Publishers, 195 Broadway, New York, NY 10007.

www.icanread.com

Library of Congress Control Number: 2001024750
ISBN 978-0-06-265526-4

Book design by Rick Farley

17 18 19 20 21   SCP   10 9 8 7 6 5 4 3 2 1   ❖   First Edition

For Holly & Tom Jaleski, with love
—M.S.

EMMETT'S PIG

Chapter One

Emmett lived in the city.

He lived in an apartment.

The apartment was in a building.

And the building was near the park.

In the park there was a zoo.

Animals lived there.

There were lions, tigers, monkeys,

camels, seals, bears, and elephants.

There were also birds and fish.

And turtles.

But no pigs.

Emmett liked pigs.

He liked them better than birds and fish.

He liked them better than

lions, tigers, monkeys, camels,

seals, bears, or elephants.

Or turtles.

"Why are there no pigs in the zoo?"

said Emmett.

"They live on farms," said his mother.

Emmett said, "Farms are in the country."

"Yes," said his father.

"Where is the country?" asked Emmett.

"The country is outside of the city."

"Is it far?" asked Emmett.

"Pretty far," said his mother.

"Oh," said Emmett.

Then he said,

"Can we go to the country someday?

Can we go to the country

and see a pig?"

"Someday," said his father.

Some animals lived

in the apartment building.

Cats and dogs lived there.

Birds and fish lived there.

And turtles.

But no pigs.

"Mother, may I have a pig
in my room?" said Emmett.
"You have more than one pig
in your room," said his mother.
"You have all your toy pigs."

Emmett did have pigs in his room.

He had bank pigs, paper pigs,

wooden pigs, and glass pigs.

He had a pink stuffed pig

with yellow button eyes.

He had pictures of pigs.

He had books about pigs.

Sometimes he had pigs in his dreams.

But he had never seen

a real live pig.

"Mother," said Emmett,

"may I have a real pig in my room?"

"No," said his mother. "I am sorry."

"Why not?" asked Emmett.

"Because pigs live on farms

where there is a lot of space

and grass and dirt."

"I could have dirt in my room,"

said Emmett.

"My pig would think it was a farm."

"But you cannot

have dirt in your room,"

said his mother.

"Oh," said Emmett.

"Can we go and live on a farm?

So that I can own a pig?"

His father shook his head.

"My job is in the city, Emmett.

I am not a farmer."

Emmett went into his room to think.

He looked at all his pigs.

He liked them very much.

But he wanted a real live pig

more than ever.

He thought and thought

and thought about it.

He could not bring a pig to live

with him in the city.

He could not go to the country

where he could own a pig.

He did not know what to do.

Emmett said to his mother and father,

"I am going to be a farmer

when I grow up.

I am going to own a lot of pigs.

When the sun goes down,

I will sit on a stump

and admire all my pigs.

My special pig

will be named King Emmett.

King Emmett will not be

with the other pigs.

King Emmett will sit by me.

He will walk around the farm with me."

"That will be fine," said his mother.

"We will come

to visit you on weekends."

Emmett was pleased.

He went in his room

to look at his calendar.

He wanted to see how many days

were left in this year.

There were a great many.

And there were a great many years left

before he could be a farmer.

But Emmett did not think

about pigs all the time.

He had to think about school.

He had to think

about playing, and about books.

He had to think

about spaceships and firemen,

and about his friends.

He had to wonder

what makes an elevator go.

He had to wonder

how many glasses of water

to ask for when he went to bed.

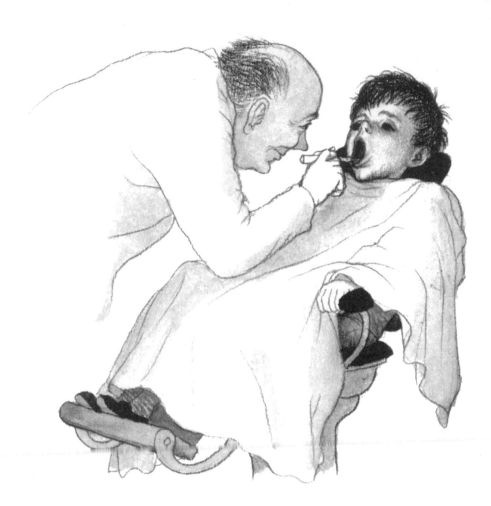

He had to go to school,

to the dentist,

to the house where his friend lived,

to the grocery store around the corner,

or just for a walk.

For a boy without a pig,

Emmett was very busy.

Chapter Two

One morning Emmett sat up in bed.

It was the thirty-first day of May.

It was Emmett's birthday.

Emmett got up and looked at his pigs

to see that they were all right.

They were all right.

He looked out of the window

to see if it was fine.

It was fine.

He went down the hall to see

if his mother and father were awake.

They were awake.

So his birthday began.

There were pancakes.

They were what Emmett liked

for a birthday breakfast.

There were present-shaped packages.

He ate the pancakes.

Then he opened the packages.

He got presents

from his two grandmothers.

He got presents

from his two grandfathers.

He got a truck and a ball and a puzzle.

He got a book to paint in.

He got a book to read.

He liked all his presents very much.

But he did not see any present

from his mother and father.

"Emmett," said his father

when the presents were all opened.

"We are going to take you

for a ride in the car."

"Yes," said his mother.

"We can call it a birthday ride.

There is a present for you at the end."

"From you?" said Emmett.

"Yes," said his mother and father.

"Can we go for the ride now?"

said Emmett.

"Right now," they said.

First they drove in the city.

"Is my present very far away?"

asked Emmett.

"Pretty far away," said his mother.

They drove through a tunnel.

"Is it in another city?" Emmett asked.

"No," said his father. "It is not."

They drove on a big highway.

"Is my present in the country?"

said Emmett.

"Yes," said his father and mother.

Emmett thought and thought.

"Is my present very small?" he asked.

"It is pretty small," said his father.

"Will it get bigger?"

"Yes," said his mother.

"It will get bigger."

41

After a long time
they turned off the highway
onto a two-lane road.
Then they turned off the two-lane road
onto a dirt road.
They turned off the dirt road
onto a driveway.
They stopped in front of a farmhouse.
A man and a woman stood
waiting and waving.

"Hello, Mr. and Mrs. Carson.

This is our son, Emmett," said his father.

"How do you do?"

said Mr. and Mrs. Carson to Emmett.

"How do you do?" said Emmett.

He looked around the farm.

He saw a garden and a stable and a silo.

He looked past the silo,

and there was a beautiful pigpen.

It was white and clean.

"Shall we walk over there?"

said Mr. Carson.

"Oh, yes," said Emmett, and he ran.

In one part of the pigpen

there was a big mother pig

and some little pigs.

One of the little pigs

looked at Emmett.

One pig had nice little hoofs,

little pointed ears,

and round happy eyes.

He was round and shiny.

He stood on his little hoofs,

his small tail curled in the air.

And he looked right up at Emmett.

Emmett stood very still for a long time.

"It is a real live pig," he said.

"A real live pig," said his father.

"Is he really mine?" said Emmett.

"He is really yours," said his mother.

"He is your birthday present.

He will live here on the farm

but he will always be your pig."

"Well," Emmett said.

"Thank you. He is just what I wanted."

"We know," said his mother and father.

"My pig is named King Emmett."

"Oh," said his father.

"You are naming your pig after yourself?"

"Yes," said Emmett.

"Only he will be King Emmett,

so as not to mix us up."

"I see," said his father.

"It is the first time

we have ever had a king

living on our farm," said Mr. Carson.

"It is the first time we ever had a pig

boarding with us," said Mrs. Carson.

Emmett smiled. He said,

"I will send him a nickel

from my allowance. For a treat."

"Fine," said Mr. Carson.

"I am sure he will enjoy that.

And I will send you

a report card about him."

"He will be good," said Emmett.

"Shall I take him out?" said Mr. Carson.

"So you can play with him?"

"Oh, yes, please," said Emmett.

So Mr. Carson lifted King Emmett
out of the pen.

King Emmett squealed.

He jumped to the grass and ran.

Emmett ran with him.

They ran all over the grass.

They ran past the silo and the stable.

They ran past the garden and the house.

Then they ran back again.

When they stopped running,

King Emmett came over

and sat down beside Emmett.

All afternoon Emmett

and his pig played together.

Now the sun was going down.

Mr. Carson put King Emmett back

with the other little pigs.

All the pigs began to eat.

Emmett sat on a stump to admire them.

Most of all he admired King Emmett.

King Emmett was the handsomest,

biggest, pinkest pig of them all.

King Emmett looked at Emmett.

"He knows you," said Mr. Carson.

"Yes," said Emmett. "He does."

Then Emmett and his mother

and father said good-bye to the Carsons

and got in their car.

They drove back to the city.

It was late when they got home.

Emmett went right to bed.

He only asked for one glass of water.

Then he went to sleep very fast,

so he could dream about King Emmett.

The next day Emmett told the teacher
and all the children in school
that he owned a pig.

He also told the elevator man,

the grocery man,

the dentist,

and a man he did not know.

They all thought it was fine.

Even the man he did not know

said it was a fine thing

to own a real live pig of your own.

Emmett was very proud.

He was also very busy.

Every week he got

a letter from Mr. Carson.

Every week he wrote back,

and sent a message to King Emmett.

Once in a while he sent

a nickel of his allowance,

so that King Emmett

could have a treat.

He had a lot of other things

to think about,

and to do.

But mostly he thought

about the day when

he and his mother and father

would all drive back

to the country to visit his pig.

And every night he had a dream.

In this dream there was

a pig and a boy.

They were both named Emmett,

and they were very good friends.

THE END

"I can read! I can read! Where are the books for me?"

One question from a young reader sparked a reading revolution!

A conversation between the director of Harper's Department of Books for Boys and Girls, Ursula Nordstrom, and Boston Public Library's Virginia Haviland inspired the I Can Read book series. Haviland told Nordstrom that a young boy had burst into the children's reading room and asked her where he could find books that were just right for a brand-new reader like himself.

Determined to fill this gap, Nordstrom published *Little Bear* by Else Holmelund Minarik, with illustrations by Maurice Sendak, in the fall of 1957. The response was immediate. According to the *New York Times*, "One look at the illustrations and children will grab for it. A second look at the short, easy sentences, the repetition of words, and the beautiful type spacing, and children will know they can read it themselves."

Delightful and wonderfully warm, *Little Bear* served as the template for the series, and now, sixty years later, we have over four hundred I Can Read stories for our youngest and newest readers!

Where the Ideas for the Characters Came From

Berenstain Bears

Stan and Jan Berenstain were cartoonists in the 1950s. When their sons began to read, they submitted a story about a family of bears to author, editor, and publisher Ted Geisel (aka Dr. Seuss), which was published as *The Big Honey Hunt* in 1962. Geisel labeled their next effort "Another Adventure of the Berenstain Bears." That's how the bears got their name!

Biscuit

One day while watching her daughter play with their neighbor's frisky dog, Alyssa Capucilli was struck by her daughter's patience and gentle nature, as well as the fact that her little girl thought the dog understood every word she said. That was the inspiration for the little yellow puppy and his sweet companion. Pat Schories's warm illustrations capture their tender relationship.

Pete the Cat

When James Dean first saw Pete, he was a tiny black kitten in a shelter. Pete looked like he had been starved and his black fur was a mess. At first, James had no interest in Pete—black cats were bad luck, after all! But the scrawny little fellow stuck his paw out of the cage, wanting to play! James took Pete home. And even though James chose to paint Pete the Cat blue (his favorite color), James realizes now that black cats are actually very good luck.

Danny and the Dinosaur

In 1958, cartoonist Syd Hoff's daughter Susan was going through a rough surgery, and one day, Syd decided to draw a picture to cheer her up. It showed a dinosaur with Syd's brother on its back. When Susie saw the picture, she exclaimed, "Danny and the dinosaur!" and that night after the family went to bed, Syd wrote the story.

Pinkalicious

Victoria Kann's daughters could never seem to get enough of cupcakes or the color pink! One year, as an April Fools' joke, Victoria told her family and friends that one of her daughters had turned pink from eating too many pink cupcakes—and so the idea for *Pinkalicious* was born!

Frog and Toad

The characters of Frog and his best friend, Toad, might have been inspired by . . . a horror movie! Arnold Lobel and his daughter, Adrianne, went to see a movie called *Frogs* at the drive-in. However, the movie featured not frogs, but toads! Adrianne told her dad about the many differences between the two—and two years later the first Frog and Toad book, *Frog and Toad Are Friends*, appeared.

Little Critter

Mercer Mayer was doodling around one day in 1974 when he drew a shape like a gourd, put two eyes on it, scribbled a nose connecting the eyes, then got coffee and forgot about it! The next day, he noticed a small piece of paper on the floor. It was his gourd. He added fuzzy hair and a big mouth; short stubby arms and feet. Mercer had created a fuzzy little "woodchuck-y porcupine" thing that became Little Critter!

Fancy Nancy

When Jane O'Connor was a small girl, every Sunday, when her grandma and great aunts came to visit, Jane would greet them at the door in a tutu and a pair of her mom's high heels. She thought she looked très glamorous!

Years later, while she was fixing dinner one night, the name Fancy Nancy flew into Jane's head, and a star made her debut!

Amelia Bedelia

Amelia Bedelia was inspired by Peggy Parish's third-grade students at the Dalton School in New York City. The children mixed up words, and Parish found them hilarious. That gave Parish the idea for Amelia Bedelia—a character who takes every word literally and embraces life with an outlook that is forthright and optimistic. Illustrator Fritz Siebel worked with Parish to create the perfect look for the conscientious cleaning lady.

Early Character Development

The Berenstain Bears

Stan and Jan Berenstain's early sketches from *The Berenstain Bears Clean House*

Pete the Cat

Frog and Toad
Early character sketch of Frog and Toad

James Dean's first painting of Pete the Cat

Biscuit

Biscuit character sketches

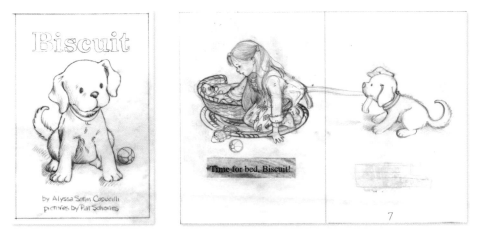

Pat Schories's early sketches from *Biscuit*

Pinkalicious

Victoria Kann's sketches for the picture book *Pinkalicious*

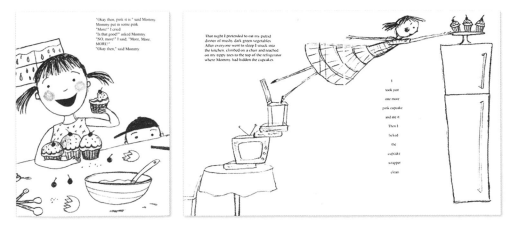

Amelia Bedelia

Fritz Siebel's sketches
for the picture book
Amelia Bedelia

Danny and the Dinosaur

Syd Hoff's early cover sketches for *Danny and the Dinosaur*

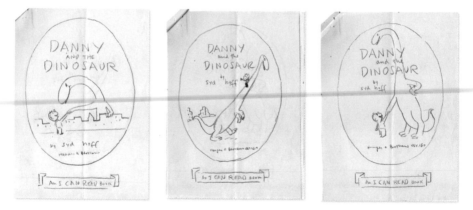

Little Critter

Mercer Mayer's early
character sketches of
Little Critter

Fancy Nancy

Robin Preiss Glasser's character sketches and cover sketch for *Fancy Nancy and the Boy from Paris*

Robert

These two catalogs marked the launch of I Can Read!

HARPER
BOOKS
for
BOYS and GIRLS
1957

HARPER
BOOKS
for
BOYS
and
GIRLS
1958

Sixty Years of *I CAN READ*

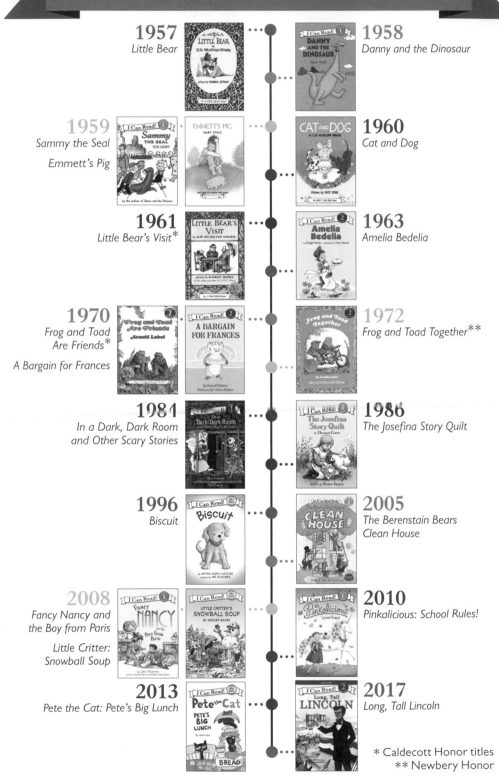

1957
Little Bear

1958
Danny and the Dinosaur

1959
Sammy the Seal

Emmett's Pig

1960
Cat and Dog

1961
Little Bear's Visit*

1963
Amelia Bedelia

1970
Frog and Toad
Are Friends*

A Bargain for Frances

1972
Frog and Toad Together**

1984
In a Dark, Dark Room
and Other Scary Stories

1986
The Josefina Story Quilt

1996
Biscuit

2005
The Berenstain Bears
Clean House

2008
Fancy Nancy and
the Boy from Paris

Little Critter:
Snowball Soup

2010
Pinkalicious: School Rules!

2013
Pete the Cat: Pete's Big Lunch

2017
Long, Tall Lincoln

* Caldecott Honor titles
** Newbery Honor